ISBN 978-1-5277-6931-1
PIBN 10889714

Forgotten Books is a registered trademark of FB &c Ltd.
Copyright © 2018 FB &c Ltd.
FB &c Ltd, Dalton House, 60 Windsor Avenue, London, SW19 2RR.
Company number 08720141. Registered in England and Wales.

For support please visit www.forgottenbooks.com

ric, archived docu

t assume content reflects c
ific knowledge, policies, or

Descriptive

Price List

Spring, 1925

THE

HOWARD-HICKORY
COMPANY

Nurserymen
Landscape Gardeners

Hickory, N. C.

Fruit Prices on Back Cover

Guarantee

The Howard-Hickory Co. exercises the greatest care possible to keep its varieties true, and holds itself in readiness to reship any trees or plants that may prove otherwise, or refund the original sum of money paid therefor, if reported to it within five years from date of order. It is mutually agreed that it is not further responsible in any case.

The Howard-Hickory Co. agrees to re-supply at half price, f. o. b. shipping point, trees and plants sold at the within-named prices that may die within one year from date of shipment from causes other than abuse or neglect, provided the account is paid promptly, and if the item is then in stock; if not, credit of like amount to be allowed on any other stock selected to take its place.

When you have us do the planting, for which there is an extra charge, any plants that die from causes other than abuse or neglect the first season will be resupplied FREE, or credited on new selection, f. o. b. Nursery, provided the original account was paid promptly.

Contents

Evergreens, Broad-leaved 10-14

Evergreens, Coniferous 15-19

Fruits ....Back Cover

Grasses, Ornamental 21

Hedge Plants 21

Peonies 10

Roses 10

Shrubs, Deciduous 1-10

Trees, Shade..19-20

Vines 21

Flowering Shrubs—Deciduous

Blooming Period

Plants arranged as to time of bloom from early spring to late summer.

Jasminum nudiflorum.
Lonicera fragrantissima.
Spirea thunbergi.
Forsythias.
Cydonia japonica.
Spiraea prunifolia.
Mahonias.
Amygdalus.
Syringas.
Cercis japonica.
Xanthorriza apiifolia.
Cercis canadensis.
Prunus, Cherry-plum.
Azalea amoena.
Azalea hinodigiri.
Cornus florida.
Cornus florida rubra.
Spiraea van houttei.
Spiraea reevesiana flore-pleno.
Deutzia lemoinei.
Deutzia gracilis.
Lonicera morrowi.
Lonicera tatarica.
Weigela.
Viburnum tomentosum plicatum.
Viburnum opulus sterile.
Eleagnus angustifolia.
Azalea lutea.
Spiraea opulifolia.
Kalmia latifolia.
Philadelphus.
Spiraea anthony waterer.
Yucca filamentosa.
Azalea arborescens.
Hydrangea arborescens grandiflora.
Azalea macrantha.
Desmodium.
Hibiscus.
Clethra alnifolia.
Hydrangea paniculata grandiflora.
Rosa rugosa.
Lagerstroemia indica.

Plants that Bloom all Summer

Abelia grandiflora.

Lonicera heckrotti.

Potentilla fruticosa.

Rosa orleans.

Flowering Shrubs, continued

Deciduous Plants For Shady Places

Berberis thunbergi.
Calycanthus floridus.
Hydrangea arborescens grandiflora.
Symphoricarpos vulgaris.
Viburnums.

Broad-Leaved Evergreens For Shady Places

Aucubas.
Ligustrums.
Mahonias.

Most of the coniferous evergreens do well in partial shade.

Plants Grown For Their Berries
Deciduous Shrubs

Callicarpa purpurea. Round, small, purple berries.

Ligustrum ibota. Oval, medium, blue-black berries.

Ilex verticillata. Round, medium, red berries.

Lonicera morrowi. Abundant medium red berries.

Lonicera tatarica. Small red berries.

Aronia arbutifolia. Small, round, red berries.

Celastrus scandens. Round, medium, yellow to red berries.

Rosa setigera. Medium, red seed pods.

Rosa rugosa. Very large, red seed pods.

Berberis thunbergi. Quantities of small red berries.

Ligustrum amurense. Many blue-black berries.

Symphoricarpos vulgaris. Drooping stems covered with red berries.

Viburnum acerfolium. Terminal bunches of bright red berries.

Viburnum dentatum. Terminal bunches of black berries.

Flowering Shrubs, continued

Evergreens With Berries

Euonymus japonica. Round red berries.
Ilex lucida. Scattered blue-black berries.
Ligustrum lucidum. Clusters of blue-black
 berries.
Ligustrum japonicum. Clusters of blue-
 black berries.
Nandina domestica. Terminal, grape-like
 clusters of red berries.

Deciduous Shrubs as to Ultimate Growth

Large

Amorpha fruticosa.
Baccharis halimifolia.
Cercis canadensis.
Cornus florida.
Crataegus coccinea.
Deutzia crenata.
Deutzia fortunei.
Deutzia Pride of Rochester.
Eleagnus angustifolia.
Forsythia fortunei.
Forsythia intermedia.
Forsythia viridissima.
Hamamelis virginica.
Hibiscus.
Lonicera fragrantissima.
Lonicera morrowi.
Lonicera tatarica.
Philadelphus coronarius.
Photinia villosa.
Rhus aromatica.
Spiraea opulifolia.
Syringa persica.
Syringa vulgaris.
Vitex agnus-castus.
Weigela candida.
Weigela rosea.

Medium

Amygdalus pumila.
Aronia arbutifolia.
Azalea lutea.
Buddleia.
Cercis chinensis.
Cornus alba sibirica.
Cornus stolonifera lutea.
Cydonia japonica.
Deutzia gracilis rosea.
Deutzia lemoinei.
Forsythia suspensa.
Hydrangea arborescens grandiflora.
Hydrangea paniculata grandiflora.

Flowering Shrubs, continued

Medium, continued

Ilex verticillata.
Ligustrum ibota.
Philadelphus bouquet blanc.
Rosa rugosa.
Rosa setigera.
Spiraea arguta.
Spiraea prunifolia.
Spiraea reevesiana fl. pl.
Spiraea van houttei.
Symphoricarpos vulgaris.
Viburnum acerfolium.
Viburnum dentatum.
Weigela Eva Rathke.

Small

Azalea arborescens.
Berberis thunbergi.
Clethra alnifolia.
Deutzia gracilis.
Desmodium.
Hypericum moserianum.
Jasminum nudiflorum.
Potentilla fruticosa.
Spiraea anthony waterer.
Spiraea thunbergi.
Xanthorriza apiifolia.

Flowering Shrubs—Deciduous

Acer palmatum. Japanese Maple, various colored foliage.
2 to 3 feet... 1.50

Amorpha fruticosa. False Indigo. Fine, feathery foliage; dark, violet-purple flowers.
3 to 4 feet... .90
4 to 5 feet... 1.25

Amygdalus pumila (Prunus japonica). Pink-flowering Almond. Double pink flowers in early spring, all along stem.
2 to 3 feet... 1.50

Amygdalus pumila alba (Prunus japonica). White-flowering Almond. Early spring.
2 to 3 feet... 1.50

Aronia arbutifolia. Red Chokeberry. Attractive for its white flowers in spring and its brilliant red berries later.
2 to 3 feet... .90
3 to 4 feet... 1.25

Azalea arborescens. Fragrant White Azalea. Large single flowers in May.
1½ to 2-foot clumps.................................. 2.50

Flowering Shrubs, continued

Azalea lutea. Great Flame Azalea.
2 to 3 feet................................. 2.50

Baccharis halimifolia. Groundsel Bush.
Late bloomer. White fluffy
flowers.
4 to 5 feet................................. 1.25

Berberis Thunbergi. Japanese Bar-
berry. Thorny; abundance of
berries in fall and winter; very
fine fall color.
1½ to 2 feet................................. .75

Buddleia. Butterfly Bush. Fragrant,
purple flowers in summer.
Heavy grower.
2-year .... .75

Caryopteris mastacanthus. Very heavy
bloomer. Blue flowers late
summer.
1½ to 2 feet................................. .90

Celastrus scandens. American Bitter-
sweet. Half-climber. Yellow
seed-capsules.
4 to 5 feet................................. 1.00

Cercis canadensis. Native Red-bud
tree.
2 to 3 feet................................. .90

Cercis chinensis (japonica). Chinese
Red-bud. Dwarfish; rose-pink
flowers in spring.
3 to 4 feet................................. 1.00

Clethra alnifolia. Summersweet. Fra-
gant white flowers in late summer.
2 to 2½ feet................................. .90

Cornus alba sibirica. Coral Dogwood.
White flowers in spring; red
twigs in winter.
2 to 3 feet................................. .90

Cornus florida. Common Dogwood.
Mass of white flowers in the
spring.
3 to 4 feet................................. 1.25
4 to 5 feet................................. 1.50

Cornus stolonifera lutea. Golden-
barked Osier Dogwood. Almost
as conspicuous in winter as is
Forsythia in the spring. Insig-
nificant white flowers in spring.
2 to 3 feet................................. 90

Crataegus coccinea. Hawthorn. Good
grower; fine fall color.
3 to 4 feet................................. 1.25

Cydonia japonica. Japanese Quince.
Abundant red flowers in early
spring. Edible fruit.
1½ to 2 feet................................. .90

Flowering Shrubs, continued

Deutzia crenata. White flowers.
2 to 3 feet.. .90

Deutzia fortunei. Very large white
flowers.
2 to 3 feet.. .90

Deutzia gracilis. Dwarf grower. Mass
of white flowers in early spring.
12 to 15 inches.................................... .90

Deutzia lemoinei. Medium grower.
White flowers.
1½ to 2 feet.. .90

Deutzia scabra. Pride of Rochester.
White flowers in June, tinged
with pink. Heavy grower.
2 to 3 feet.. .75

Desmodium. Drooping branches, covered with rose-purple flowers in
summer.
2-year.. .75

Eleagnus angustifolia. Russian Olive.
Foliage light green above, sil-
very beneath; rapid grower.
4 to 5 feet.. 1.25

Euonymus alatus. Winged burning-
bush. Brilliant fall coloring.
Red berries.
3 to 4 feet.. 2.50
4 to 5 feet.. 3.00

Forsythia fortunei. Fortune's Gold-
en Bell.
2 to 3 feet.. .90

Forsythia intermedia. Hybrid Golden
Bell. Medium grower.
2 to 3 feet.. .90

Forsythia suspensa. Drooping Golden
Bell.
2 to 3 feet.. .90

Forsythia viridissima. Golden Bell.
Habit erect.
2 to 3 feet.. .90

Hamamelis virginica. Native Witch
Hazel.
1½ to 2 feet.. .90

Hibiscus (Althea; Rose of Sharon).
Summer bloomer.
2 to 3 feet.. .90

Anemonaeflorus. Rose or purple
with dark base.

Ardens. Double; purple.

Boule de Feu. Double; red.

Lady Stanley. Double: white, crim-
son center.

Paeoniflorus. White with dark center

Totus Albus. Single white.

Flowering Shrubs, continued

Hydrangea arborescens grandiflora, Hills of Snow. Flat, white blooms in summer.
1½ to 2 feet................................ .90

Hydrangea paniculata. Large, creamy white flowers in late summer.
3 to 4 feet................................ .90

Hydrangea paniculata grandiflora. Large, white conical flowers, bronzing in fall; somewhat larger than Paniculata.
2 to 3 feet................................ .90

Hypericum aureum. Taller than Hypericum moserianum. Golden flowers.
2 or 3 feet................................ .90

Hypericum moserianum. Dwarf; large single, yellow flowers in summer.
Clumps................................ .90

Ilex verticillata. Winterberry. Red berries in fall and into January.
2½ to 3 feet................................ 1.00

Jasminum nudiflorum. January Jasmine. Willowy limbs, covered with yellow flowers before leaves appear.
1½ to 2 feet................................ .75
2 to 3 feet................................ .90

Jasminum primulinum. Chinese jasmine. Yellow blooms; nearly an evergreen.
2 to 3 feet................................ 1.50

Lagerstroemia indica. Crape Myrtle. Beautiful flowers in late summer; red, rose pink.
2 to 3 feet................................ 1.25
3 to 4 feet................................ 1.50
4 to 5 feet................................ 2.50
5 to 6 feet................................ 4.00

Ligustrum ibota regelianum. Regel's Privet. Blue-black berries in fall.
3 to 4-foot spread................................ 1.50

Lonicera fragrantissima. Early Fragrant Honeysuckle. Free grower.
2 to 3 feet................................ 1.25

Lonicera grandiflora rosea. Bush Honeysuckle; rose flowers.
2 to 3 feet................................ .90

Lonicera Morrowi. Bush Honeysuckle. White flowers in spring; red berries in summer and fall.
2 to 3 feet................................ .90
3 to 4 feet................................ 1.00

Flowering Shrubs, continued

Lonicera tatarica. Bush Honeysuckle. Pink flowers, followed by red berries.
2 to 3 feet... .90

Peony. 3 to 5 eyes.................................. 1.00

Philadelphus coronarius. Sweet Syringa.
2 to 3 feet... .75
3 to 4 feet... .90

Philadelphus coronarius grandiflorus. Large single white flowers.
2 to 3 feet... .75
3 to 4 feet... .90

Philadelphus Bouquet Blanc. Medium grower. White, fragrant flowers.
2 to 3 feet... 1.00

Photinia villosa. White flowers in June. Heavy grower. Red berries.
5 to 6 feet, heavy................................ 2.50

Potentilla fruticosa. Silver gray foliage; continuous bloomer, bright yellow; grows almost any location; dwarfish.
15 to 18 inches .... .90

Rhus aromatica. Fragrant Sumac. Fragrant odor from crushed leaves. Beautiful fall color.
2 to 3 feet... 1.00
3 to 4 feet... 1.25

Rosa. Rose; 2 yr, field grown............ 1.00

Rosa rugosa. Rugose or rough foliage; red or white flowers followed by red fruit. Gorgeous fall coloring.
1½ to 2 feet... .75
2 to 3 feet... .90

Rosa setigera. Prairie Rose. Arching habit; free growth. Red single flowers in May. Red fruit.
3 to 4 feet... 1.50

Spiraea arguta. Medium grower; white flowers in spring. Feathery foliage.
2 to 3 feet... .75

Spiraea anthony waterer. Dwarf, bright red flowers all summer if pruned.
1½ to 2 feet... 1.00
2 to 2½ feet... 1.25

Spiraea reevesiana fl.-fl. Heavy umbels of white flowers in early summer.
4 to 6 feet... 1.50

Flowering Shrubs, continued

Spiraea prunifolia fl.-pl. Bridal Wreath. Stems loaded with double white flowers in spring.
3 to 4 feet.. .90

Spiraea Reevesiana fl.-fl. Heavy bloomer. Double white flowers in spring.
2 to 3 feet.................................... .90

Spiraea thunbergi. Dwarf. Mass of white flowers in early spring.
15 to 18 inches.......................... .75

Spiraea van houttei. Drooping growth; white flowers in spring.
2 to 3 feet.................................... .75
3 to 4 feet.................................... .90

Symphoricarpos vulgaris. Coralberry. Stems drooping and covered with red berries in fall and early winter.
2 to 3 feet.................................... .60
3 to 4 feet.................................... .75

Syringa persica. Persian Purple Lilac. Good bloomer; fine foliage.
2 to 3 feet.................................... 1.00
3 to 4 feet.................................... 1.25

Syringa vulgaris... Common Purple Lilac.
2 to 3 feet.................................... .75

Syringa vulgaris alba. Common White Lilac.
1½ to 2 feet................................. .90

Viburnum acerfolium. Maple-leaved Viburnum. Good in shady locations; white flowers in June followed by red berries.
2 to 3 feet.................................... 1.00

Viburnum dentatum. Arrowwood. Good in shady locations; glossy green leaves; black berries.
3 to 4 feet.................................... .90

Viburnum opulus nanum. Dwarf Snowball. Good foliage for borders.
8 to 10 inches............................. .75

Viburnum opulus sterile. Old-fashioned Snowball. Grows almost anywhere and flowers abundantly.
2 to 3 feet.................................... 90

Vitex agnus-castus. Hemp-tree. Lilac colored, fragrant flowers in terminal clusters in late summer.
2 to 3 feet.................................... .90

Weigela Eva Rathke. Red flowers in summer.
1½ to 2 feet................................. 1.25

Flowering Shrubs, continued

Weigela nana variegata. Rose flowers
in early summer; golden tinted
foliage.
2 to 3 feet.................................... .90
3 to 4 feet.................................... 1.00

Weigela rosea. Rose flowers in summer; very heavy grower.
3 to 4 feet.................................... 1.00

Xanthorrhiza apiifolia. Yellow-Root.
Good foliaged ground-cover.
1½ to 2 feet.............................. .75

PEONIES. 3 to 5 eyes.................. 1.00

ROSES. 2-year, field grown................ 1.00

Broad-Leaved Evergreens

With the exception of Magnolia grandiflora, which makes a tall tree, and Pachysandra terminalis, which is a ground-cover,
almost all Broad-leaved Evergreens are
suitable for mass plantings. Most of them
do well in partial shade, and can be kept
to almost any height by pruning.

As to Ultimate Growth

Large Bushy

Escallonia macrantha rosea.
Euonymus japonica.
Ilex opaca (tree.)
Laurocerasus carolinianum.
Laurocerasus officinalis.
Ligustrum japonicum.
Ligustrum quihoui.
Lonicera fragrantissima.
Viburnum rhytidophyllum.

Medium

Abelia grandiflora.
Aucuba.
Berberis illicifolia.
Buxus.
Euonymus sieboldi.
Ilex crenata.
Ilex lucida.
Kalmia latifolia.
Ligustrum aureum.
Ligustrum lucidum.
Ligustrum nepalense.
Lonicera nitida.
Mahonia aquifolium.
Mahonia japonica.
Nandina domestica.
Viburnum tinus.

Broad-Leaved Evergreens, continued

Small

Azalea amoena.
Azalea hinodigiri.
Azalea macranthus.
Euonymus japonicus microphyllus.
Hypericum calycinum.
Pachysandra terminalis (groundcover).
Yucca filamentosa.

Broad-leaved Evergreens ought to be used freely around our homes. No class of shrubs is better adapted to foundation plantings, for groups at the entrance, or curves in the driveway, or for massing in front of taller cone-bearing evergreens. We would like to see a group of Broad-leaves around every southern home.

Abelia grandiflora. Pinkish white, bell-shaped flowers from June to frost.
1 to 1½ feet...$1.00
1½ to 2 feet.. 1.25
2 to 3 feet.. 1.50

Andromeda (Pieris) japonica. Japanese Fetterbush. Waxy white flowers in early spring.
12 to 15 inches................................... 2.50

Aucuba japonica aurea maculata. Gold Dust Plant. Large green leaves with golden spots. Requires partial shade.
12 to 15 inches................................... 2.00
15 to 18 inches 3.00
1½ to 2 feet...................................... 4.00
2 to 2½ feet...................................... 5.00

Azalea amoena. Dwarf, bushy shrub with coppery green leaves and dark pink flowers in early spring.
10 to 12-inch spread-height............. 3.00

Azalea hinodigiri. Vivid red flowers in spring. Bushy; good green foliage.
10 to 12-inch spread-height............. 3.00
12 to 15-inch spread-height............. 4.00

Azalea macranthus. Very large single red blooms. Striking when in flower.
10 to 12-inch spread-height............. 3.00

Berberis illicifolia. Holly-leaved Barberry.
2 to 2½ feet...................................... 3.00

Berberis Wilsonae.
12 to 15 inch..................................... 2.00

Broad-Leaved Evergreens, continued

Buxus sempervirens. Common Tree Box.

1½ to 2 feet.. 4.00
2 to 2½ feet.. 5.00

Buxus sempervirens pyramidalis. Pyramidal Tree Box.

12 to 15 inches 2.00
15 to 18 inches................................. 3.50
1½ to 2 feet..................................... 5.00

Cotoneaster buxifolia. Abundance of red berries.

1½ to 2-foot spread-height............... 3.00

Escallonia macrantha rosea. Large spreading; finely serrate, rough leaves; terminal racemes of pink flowers.

1½ to 2 feet..................................... 2.00

Euonymus carrieri. Dwarf compact growth.

12 to 15 inches................................ 1.00

Euonymus japonicus. Red berrries in fall and winter. Dark green foliage.

2 to 2½ feet..................................... 3.00
2½ to 3 feet..................................... 4.00
• 3 to 3½ feet................................... 5.00

Euonymus japonicus microphyllus. Very dwarfish.

12 to 15 inches................................ 3.00
15 to 18 inches................................ 4.00

Euonymus radicans. Good foliage.

2½ to 3 feet, bush form.................... 5.00

Euonymus radicans marginatum. Green foliage with white margins.

1½ to 2 feet.....................................2.50
2 to 2½ feet..................................... 3.50

Euonymus sieboldi. Brilliant red seed pods. Drops its foliage in some sections.

2½ to 3 feet..................................... 5.00

Hypericum calycinum. Aaron's Beard. Attains only about a height of 1½ feet; large, showy, orange-yellow flowers with large stamens.

Clumps 1.00

Ilex crenata. Japanese Holly. Leaves very similar to Common Tree Box. Black berries.

1½ to 2 feet..................................... 4.00
2 to 2½ feet..................................... 4.50
2½ to 3 feet..................................... 5.00
3 to 3½ feet..................................... 6.00

Broad-Leaved Evergreens, continued

Ilex lucida. Erect growth.
　2 to 3 feet.................................... 2.00

Kalmia latifolia.   Mountain Laurel.
　Flowers in early spring.
　2 to 2½ feet.................................. 4.00

Laurocerasus caroliniana.   Carolina
　Cherry; Cherry Laurel.   White
　flowers;   black berries.   Tall
　grower.
　2 to 3 feet.................................... 3.00
　3 to 4 feet.................................... 4.00

Laurocerasus officinalis.   English
　Laurel.   Long, broad, dark
　green leaves; heavy growth.
　15 to 18 inches............................ 4.00
　18 to 24 inches............................ 5.00

Ligustrum aureum.   Manda's Golden
　Privet.
　1½ to 2 feet.................................. 2.50

Ligustrum japonicum. Japanese Priv-
　et.   Rapid grower.   White
　flowers; blue-black berries.
　1½ to 2 feet.................................. 2.00
　2 to 3 feet.................................... 3.00
　3 to 4 feet.................................... 4.00

Ligustrum lucidum. Dark bottle-green
　foliage; white flowers, black
　berries.
　1½ to 2 feet.................................. 3.00
　2 to 3 feet.................................... 4.00

Ligustrum nepalense.   Smaller leaf
　than above; more upright.
　2 to 3 feet.................................... 4.00

Ligustrum quihoui. The latest flow-
　ering Ligustrum.   Blue-black
　berries. Drops it foliage parti-
　ally.
　2 to 3 feet.................................... 2.00
　3 to 4 feet.................................... 3.00

Lonicera fragrantissima. First Breath
　of Spring.
　2 to 3 feet.................................... 1.25

Lonicera nitida.   Medium grower.
　Good foliage.
　15 to 18 inches............................ 2.50
　1½ to 2 feet.................................. 3.50
　2 to 2½ feet.................................. 5.00

Lonicera pileata. Dwarf.
　15 to 18 inches............................ 3.00

Mahonia aquifolium.   Oregon Holly-
　grape.   Yellow flowers in
　spring; blue berries.
　15 to 18 inches spread-height........ 3.00

Broad-Leaved Evergreens, continued

Mahonia japonica. Japanese Mahonia.
Yellow flowers; blue berries.

15 to 18 inches	3.00
1½ to 2 feet	4.00
2 to 2½ feet	5.00

Nandina domestica. Japanese Nandina. Upright-growing, numerous reed-like stems; foliage glossy green tinged with red, which assumes beautiful coppery red tones in winter; white flowers followed by bright red berries, which are retained till after Christmas.

1½ to 2 feet	3.00
2 to 2½ feet	4.00
2½ to 3 feet	5.00

Pachysandra terminalis. A ground cover.

2-year	.50

Viburnum rhytidophyllum. Yellowish white flowers, red berries.

2 to 2½ feet	3.50
3 to 3½ feet	5.00

Viburnum tinus. Very dark green leaves; white flowers.

1½ to 2 feet	4.00
2 to 2½ feet	5.00

Yucca filamentosa. Adam's Needle. Long spikes of white flowers in June.

2-year	.75

Trustworthy Trees & Plants
Members
American Association of Nurserymen
Southern Nurserymen's Asso.

To make America more fruitful and beautiful should be the ambition of every loyal Southerner. It can be done if you will help. It does not mean that you must spend a lot of money, but it does mean that you should have some fruit trees and berries in your home garden; that your house be made cooler in summer by some shade trees, and that a few flowering shrubs give color from spring to fall. A little from every one makes a beautiful town for all.

Coniferous Evergreens
As to Ultimate Growth
Trees

Cedrus deodora.
Juniperus japonica sylvestris.
Juniperus oblonga pendula.
Juniperus virginiana.
Juniperus virginiana glauca.
Picea excelsa.
Picea pungens.
Pinus sylvestris.
Thuja occidentalis.
Thuja occidentalis Lobbi.
Thuja orientalis.

Medium Grower

Juniperus excelsa stricta.
Juniperus hibernica.
Retinospora obtusa compacta.
Retinospora filifera.
Retinospora plumosa.
Retinospora plumosa aurea.
Retinospora squarrosa veitchi.
Thuja occidentalis filicodes.
Thuja occidentalis pyramidalis.
Thuja orientalis compacta.
Thuja orientalis Rosedale.
Thuja orientalis semi-glauca.
Thuja orientalis pyramidalis.

Smaller

Juniperus japonica.
Juniperus pfitzeriana.
Juniperus nana.
Juniperus sabina.
Juniperus sabina tamariscifolia (almost
    flat.)
Thuja occidentalis conica densa.
Thuja occidentalis ellwangeriana.
Thuja occidentalis globosa.
Thuja occidentalis Hoveyi.
Thuja occidentalis wareana.
Thuja orientalis aurea nana.

T signifies plants that can be used in tubs, urns, boxes, etc.

S signifies that the plant is usually used as a specimen.

M signifies that the variety is often used for mass planting around foundation, in corners of the lawn, etc.

It is to be remembered, however, that either or all may be used in combination in landscape work. Junipers and Retinosporas can be kept to almost any desired size or shape by judicious pruning. Thujas (Arborvitaes) can be pruned sparingly.

Coniferous Evergreens, continued

Cedrus deodora. Indian Cedar.
2 to 3 feet.. 5.00

Juniperus chinensis Pfitzeriana. Pfitzer's Juniper. Semi-spreading; grey-green. M.
12 to 15-inch spread........................ 3.00
15 to 18-inch spread........................ 4.00

Juniperus hibernica. Irish Juniper. Upright; columnar. S.
1½ to 2 feet................................. 2.50
2 to 2½ feet................................. 3.00
3 to 3½ feet................................. 5.00

Juniperus excelsa stricta. Broadly pyramidal.
15 to 18 inches.............................. 3.00
1½ to 2 feet................................. 3.50
2 to 2½ feet................................. 4.00
2½ to 3 feet................................. 5.00
3 to 3½ feet................................. 6.00

Juniperus japonica. Dark green. Open growth.
15 to 18 inches spread height........... 2.50
18 to 24 inches spread-height........... 3.00

Juniperus japonica sylvestris. Pyramidal, dense, bluish.
2 to 3 feet................................... 4.00
3 to 4 feet................................... 5.00

Juniperus nana. Vase-shaped growth. Mixed grey, green foliage.
1½ to 2-foot spread......................... 4.00

Juniperus oblonga pendula. Medium height; drooping branches; dark green foliage. S.
5 to 6 feet................................... 7.50

Juniperus Sabina. Savin Juniper. Bushy; semi-erect; dark green foliage M.
15 to 18-inch spread........................ 3.00
1½ to 2-foot spread......................... 4.00

Juniperus sabina tamariscifolia. Tamarix-leaved Savin Juniper. Low, spreading; foliage, mixed green and grey. M.
1½ to 2 feet................................. 4.00

Juniperus virginiana. Virginia Red Cedar. Tall. S.
2½ to 3 feet................................. 3.50
3 to 3½ feet................................. 4.00
3½ to 4 feet................................. 5.00
4 to 4½ feet................................. 6.00

Juniperus virginiana glauca. Blue Virginia Cedar.
2 to 2½ feet................................. 5.00
2½ to 3 feet................................. 6.00
4 to 4½ feet................................. 7.50

Coniferous Evergreens, continued

Picea excelsa. Norway Spruce. Tall grower; standard tree type. S.

1½ to 2 feet	2.50
2 to 2½ feet	3.00
3 to 3½ feet	4.00
3½ to 4 feet	5.00
4½ to 5 feet	7.00

Picea pungens. Colorado Spruce.

1½ to 2 feet	4.00

Pinus sylvestris. Scotch Pine.

1½ to 2 feet	3.00

Retinospora obtusa compacta. Dwarfish; dark green foliage. M.

1½ to 2 feet	4.00

Retinospora filifera. Thread-branched. Dwarfish; drooping. M.

2½ to 3 feet	7.50
3 to 3½ feet	9.00
3½ to 4 feet	10.00

Retinospora plumosa. Plume-like. Medium grower. M.S.

1½ to 2 feet	4.00
2 to 2½ feet	5.00
2½ to 3 feet	6.50
3 to 3½ feet	7.50

Retinospora plumosa aurea. Golden Plume-like. M. S.

1½ to 2 feet	4.50
2½ to 3 feet	7.50

Retinospora squarrosa seiboldi. Dwarfish; fluffy, soft blue foliage. Bronze in Winter. M. S.

3 to 4 feet	7.50

Retinospora veitchi. Fluffy grey foliage. M. S.

15 to 18-inches	3.00
1½ to 2 feet	4.50
2 to 2½ feet	6.00

Taxus baccata repanda. Spreading English Yew. M.

1½ to 2-foot spread	5.00

Taxus cuspidata. Japanese Yew. Upright, rather open growth. M. S.

2 to 2½ feet	6.00

Taxus cuspidata brevifolia. Dwarf Japanese Yew. Irregular, unique outline. M.

1½ to 2 feet	6.00

Taxus cuspidata capitata. M.

2 to 2½ feet	6.00

Coniferous Evergreens, continued

Thuja occidentalis. American Arborvitae. Erect, somewhat pyramidal, free grower. S. M.
2 to 2½ feet..................................... 3.00
2½ to 3 feet.................................... 4.00
3 to 4 feet...................................... 5.00
4 to 5 feet...................................... 6.50
6 to 7 feet...................................... 9.00
7 to 8 feet...................................... 12.00

Thuja occidentalis Ellwangeriana. Tom
Thumb Arborvitae. Low, spreading; fluffy, soft foliage. M. T.
15 to 18-inch spread..................... 3.00
18 to 24-inch spread 4.00

Thuja occidentalis filicoides. Fern-
like pyramidal Arborvitae, medium grower. S. M.
1½ to 2 feet.................................. 3.50
2 to 2½ feet.................................. 4.00
2½ to 3 feet.................................. 6.00

Thuja occidentalis globosa. Globe
Arborvitae. M. S. T.
15 to 18 inches............................... 3.00

Thuja occidentalis lobbi. Lobb's American Arborvitae. Tall, open
growth. S.
3½ to 4 feet................................. 4.00
4 to 4½ feet................................. 5.00

Thuja occidentalis pyramidalis. Pyramidal American Arborvitae.
M. S.
1½ to 2 feet.................................. 3.50
2 to 2½ feet.................................. 5.00
2½ to 3 feet.................................. 6.00
3 to 3½ feet................................. 7.50

Thuja occidentalis wareana. Siberian
Arborvitae. Slow growing; compact, somewhat pyramidal habit;
dark rich green foliage. S.
15 to 18 inches 3.00
1½ to 2 feet.................................. 4.00

Thuja orientalis. Chinese Arborvitae.
Free, open growth. S.
2½ to 3 feet.................................. 3.50
3 to 3½ feet.................................. 4.00
3½ to 4 feet................................. 5.00
4 to 5 feet.................................... 6.00
5 to 6 feet.................................... 7.00

Thuja orientalis aurea nana. Dwarf
Golden Arborvitae. Very formal.
M. S. T.
1½ to 2 feet.................................. 6.00

Thuja orientalis compacta. Formal;
medium growth. M. S. T.
2 to 2½ feet................................. 4.00
2½ to 3 feet................................. 6.00

Coniferous Evergreens, continued

Thuja orientalis pyramidalis.
2 to 2½ feet.. 4.00
3 to 3½ feet.. 7.00

Thuja orientalis, Rosedale. Compact
growth. Fluffy blue foliage.
2 to 2½ feet.. 5.00
2½ to 3 feet.. 6.00
3 to 3½ feet.. 7.00

Thuja orientalis semi-glauca. Pyramidal growth. Blue foliage.
2 to 2½ feet.. 5.00
2½ to 3 feet.. 6.00
3 to 3½ feet.. 7.00

Tsuga caroliniana. Carolina Hemlock.
Medium, compact growth. S. M.
1½ to 2 feet.. 4.00
2 to 2½ feet.. 5.00
2½ to 3 feet.. 6.00
3 to 4 feet.. 7.00
4 to 5 feet.. 8.00

Shade and Ornamental Trees

Acer dasycarpum. Silver Maple.
Very light foliage.
8 to 10 feet..$2.50
10 to 12 feet.. 3.25
12 to 14 feet.. 4.00
14 to 16 feet.. 5.00

Acer platanoides. Norway Maple.
Dark green foliage; roundish
symmetrical head.
8 to 10 feet.. 4.00
10 to 12 feet, 1¾ to 2-inch cal 6.00
10 to 12 feet, 2 to 2¼-inch cal........ 7.50
12 to 14 feet, 2½ to 3-inch cal........10.00

Acer saccharum... Sugar maple. Very
tall grower, stately. The fall
coloring is simply gorgeous.
7 to 8 feet.. 2.50
8 to 10 feet.. 3.00
10 to 12 feet.. 4.00
12 to 14 feet.. 5.00

Catalpa bungei. Small umbrella-type
tree. 3 year head.
5 to 6 feet.. 5.00

Ginkgo biloba (Salisburia adiantifolia)
Maidenhair Tree. Something
different.
7 to 8 feet.. 3.00
8 to 10 feet.. 4.00
10 to 12 feet.. 6.00

Lagerstroemia indica. Crape Myrtle.
5 to 6 feet 4.00

Magnolia grandiflora. Evergreen.
Large, fragrant white flowers.
4 to 5 feet.. 4.00

Shade and Ornamental Trees, continued

Melia azedarach umbraculiformis.
Texas umbrella tree. Subject
to winter-kill in some sections.
2 to 3 feet.................................... 1.00
3 to 4 feet.................................... 1.50

Populus berolinensis. Volga Poplar.
Fast grower; more spreading
than Lombardy.
8 to 10 feet.................................... 2.50

Populus nigra fastigiata. Lombardy
Poplar. Quick grower; colum-
nar.
8 to 10 feet.................................... 2.50

Prunus. Compass Cherry-Plum.
3 to 4 feet.................................... 1.50

Quercus nigra (aquatica). Water Oak.
Narrow leaves.
8 to 10 feet.................................... 5.00
10 to 12 feet.................................... 6.00

Quercus palustris. Pin Oak. Symmetrical broad pyramidal crown;
drooping branches.
8 to 10 feet, 1½ to 1¾-inch cal.... 4.00
10 to 12 feet, 2 to 2¼-inch cal.... 6.00
12 to 14 feet, 2½ to 3-inch cal........ 9.00

Quercus phellos. Willow Oak.
7 to 8 feet.................................... 4.00
8 to 10 feet.................................... 5.00

Salix caprea. Pussy Willow.
3 to 4 feet.................................... 1.50

Tilia americana. American Linden;
Basswood. Good grower; large
heartshaped leaves.
10 to 12 feet, 1¾ to 2-inch cal........ 5.00
12 to 14 feet, 2 to 2½-inch 7.00

Ulmus americana. American White
Elm. Heads high; fine for
street tree.
7 to 8 feet.................................... 1.50
8 to 10 feet.................................... 2.00
10 to 12 feet.................................... 3.00

Walnut, Black.
3 to 4 feet.................................... 1.00

Landscape Service

In this department you are rendered
complete service; not only can we supply
you with the plants, but tell you how they
should be used to best advantage, and then
actually set them in their proper locations.
Write us for further particulars; your suc-
cess is assured.

Vines
Deciduous

Ampelopsis quinquefolia. Virginia Creeper. Heavy foliage; wonderful fall color.
4-year.. .75

Ampelopsis quinquefolia engelmanni. Finer cut foliage than above.
4-year.. .75

Ampelopsis tricuspidata veitchi. Boston Ivy. Brilliant red fall color.
4-year.. .75

Celastrus scandens. American Bittersweet. Abundance of berries, yellow and red.
4 to 5 feet................................ 1.00

Lonicera heckrotti. Vine Honeysuckle with red flowers all summer.
2-year.. 1.00

Wistaria sinensis. Purple Wistaria. Bears long clusters of purple flowers.
2-year.. 1.00

Wistaria sinensis alba.
2 to 3 feet............................... 1.00

Evergreen

All evergreen vines below cling to walls of brick and stone when the surface is fairly rough.

Euonymus radicans. Narrow leaves.
4-year.. 1.50

Euonymus radicans vegetus. Broadleaved. Berries.
2 to 2½ feet............................ 2.50

Euonymus radicans marginatum. Leaves with golden margins.
1½ to 2 feet............................ 2.50
2 to 2½ feet............................ 3.50

Hedera helix. English Ivy. Glossy, green, heavy foliage.
2-year .... .75

Ornamental Grasses

Eulalia japonica gracillima. Green in color. Heavy grower.
Clumps....................................$1.50

Eulalia japonica variegata. Yellow foliage.
Clumps 1.50

Hedge Plants

Ligustrum amurense. Amoor River Privet. Evergreen.
2 to 3 feet, per 100...................$10.00
(Privet is always cut back to about six inches before shipping.)
100 Shrubs for hedges at 10 per cent. discount from "each" rate.

It's not a farm Home Without Fruit

The Howard-Hickory Co.

Nurserymen
Landscape Gardeners

HICKORY, NORTH CAROLINA

FRUIT DEPARTMENT

APPLE, 4 to 5 feet, 1 and 2 yr............$0.60
  Special .... .75
APRICOT 1.00
CHERRY 1.25
FIG .... .60
GRAPE, Bunch kinds.................... .50
  Scuppernong family .... .75
MULBERRY 1.00
PEACH, 4 to 5 feet.................... .50
  3 to 4 feet.................... .40
  Special .... .75
  4 to 5 feet per 100 ....$30
  3 to 4 feet per 100..............$26
  2 to 3 feet per 100..............$22
PEAR 1.00
PECAN. 3 to 4 feet.................... 1.75
  4 to 5 feet 2.50
  5 to 6 feet.................... 3.00
PERSIMMON, Japanese 1.00
PLUM and DAMSON.................... 1.00
WALNUT, Black 1.00
BLACKBERRY, doz. 2.00
DEWBERRY, doz. 2.00
RASPBERRY, doz. 2.00
STRAWBERRY, per 100 .... 2.00
  per 1000 ....10.00
ROSES 1.00

Discounts on Fruits Besides Peach.
  10 per cent on 50 trees.
  20 per cent on 100 trees.

CPSIA information can be obtained
at www.ICGtesting.com
Printed in the USA
BVHW090027211118
533618BV00023B/3300/P